# SCIENCE WORKS

# UP, DOWN, ALL AROUND

## A STORY OF GRAVITY

Jacqui Bailey  Matthew Lilly

Picture Window Books • Minneapolis, Minnesota

Editor: Jacqueline A. Wolfe
Page Production: Melissa Kes
Creative Director: Keith Griffin
Editorial Director: Carol Jones

First American edition published in 2006 by
Picture Window Books
5115 Excelsior Boulevard
Suite 232
Minneapolis, MN  55416
1-877-845-8392
www.picturewindowbooks.com

First published in Great Britain by
A & C Black Publishers Limited
37 Soho Square, London  W1D 3QZ
Copyright © Two's Company 2003

Printed in the United States of America.

**Library of Congress Cataloging-in-Publication Data**
Bailey, Jacqui.
Up, down, all around : a story of gravity / by Jacqui Bailey ; illustrated by Matthew Lilly.
p. cm. — (Science works)
Includes bibliographical references and index.
ISBN 1-4048-1597-X
1.  Gravity—Juvenile literature. 2.  Gravitation—Juvenile literature.  I. Lilly, Matthew, ill. II. Title.
QC178.B278 2006                    531'.14—dc22

With many thanks to astronomer Carole Stott for her help.

For Chris
JB

For Finola, Holly, and Bill
ML

Special thanks to our advisers for their expertise, research, and advice:

Larry M. Browning, Ph.D., Professor, Physics Department
South Dakota State University, Brookings, South Dakota, USA

Dr. Robin Armstrong, Peter Tandy, and Charlotte Stockley
Mineralogy Department at the Natural History Museum
London, England

Susan Kesselring, M.A., Literacy Educator,
Rosemount-Apple Valley-Eagan (Minnesota) School District

Zac leapt out of bed and his feet thudded to the ground. Today was THE DAY!

He hummed to himself as the hot shower water splashed down over his head.

MMM MM MMM MM...

HMM HMM HUM HUM...

He went on humming as he cleaned his teeth and pulled on his jeans and a T-shirt.

DA DEE DEE DA!

He was too excited to eat. He grabbed his keys and jacket and headed out the door.

Hang on! Let's stop a minute and think about the things Zac has just done.

When you jump out of bed in the morning, have you ever wondered what keeps your feet on the ground? Or why water always flows downward when you turn on a shower or a tap?

Or why, when you throw a ball in the air, it always falls toward the ground?

The answer is a mysterious, natural force called gravity.

Nobody really knows what gravity is, but everyone can feel it. It's there all the time, pulling you and everything else toward the center of the earth.

The way gravity works was first described using math in the 1660s by a scientist named Isaac Newton. He is supposed to have had the idea after he was hit on the head by a falling apple, but no one knows if it really happened that way.

Gravity keeps your feet on the ground. It's why things roll downhill or fall when you let them go. Without it, everything that isn't attached to the ground would float away—and so would the air we breathe and the water in the oceans.

The drive to work didn't take long. Zac parked his car and headed for the main office. Everyone was busy and bustling around. It was always like that on launch day, but today was even more special for Zac. Today he was making his first flight into space.

Zac had been training to be an astronaut for years. He had worked hard to keep himself fit.

He had gone through all kinds of physical tests to make sure his body could cope with the difficulties of being in space. When in orbit, gravity keeps Zac, the shuttle, and everything in it in orbit around Earth. Because everything is falling with Zac, there is nothing to counteract the pull of gravity.

He had learned how to work in a spacesuit by wearing one underwater.

Being underwater is a little like being in space. There is no air to breathe, and things float around.

TURN TO PAGE 2,039 IN YOUR MANUAL...

He had been taught everything there was to know about how the space shuttle worked, and now he was ready to go.

Zac changed into his work clothes and met up with the rest of the crew for breakfast. They were all excited, even though some of them had been into space before.

Zac knew he had hours to wait before the launch—that wouldn't happen until much later.

In the meantime, the medical staff gave the crew a final check-up to make sure they were still healthy and recorded their weight.

What we call "weight" is actually gravity pulling down on all the stuff that makes up your body.

When scientists talk about how much stuff something is made of—whether it's a feather, an elephant, or you—they use the word "mass."

Mass is not the same as size. Something can be small and heavy because it has a lot of mass. An apple is heavier than a balloon, for example, because it has more mass than the balloon.

At last, it was time for the flight crew to board the shuttle. One of the ground crew strapped Zac into his seat and gave him a thumbs up and asked, "Are you OK?"

Zac nodded nervously.

The crew waited while the final checks were made. Then the shuttle's rockets roared into action and everything shook as it lifted off the launch pad.

HERE WE GO ...

The spacecraft has to travel fast enough and far enough to get above Earth's atmosphere (the air that surrounds Earth) and go into orbit.

WHAT WAS THAT?

This means it must reach a speed of a more than 17,000 miles (28,000 kilometers) per hour—three times faster than the fastest aircraft—to climb almost 186 miles (300 km) above Earth's surface. To do this, the shuttle has to ride piggy-back on a pair of very powerful booster rockets.

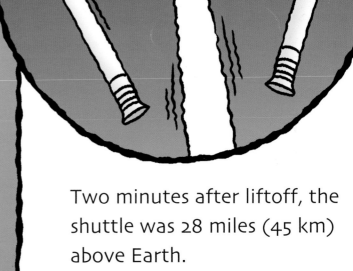

Two minutes after liftoff, the shuttle was 28 miles (45 km) above Earth.

**BANG! BANG!**

The two booster rockets were used up. They dropped away and fell back to Earth.

13

The shuttle went faster and faster. It was speeding up so quickly it made Zac feel three times heavier than normal. He felt as if a giant hand was pressing him into his seat.

The main engine shut down, and a few seconds later there was another loud bang. This time, the giant fuel tank fell away.

BANG!

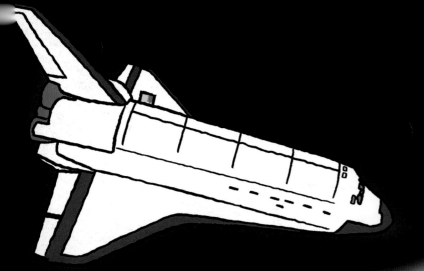

Small rockets in the tail hissed as they boosted the shuttle even higher. Then suddenly, everything went quiet. Zac was in space.

Everyone breathed a sigh of relief and released their seatbelts. Zac floated up from his seat and his head touched the ceiling.

Someone bumped into him and he felt himself bounce away toward the opposite wall.

"Sorry," said Anna.

Zac reached for a strap to hold on to. He was feeling a bit spacesick, but he knew it wouldn't last. It was just his body getting used to being weightless.

ISN'T THIS GREAT?

I THINK I'M GOING TO BE SICK.

When you are in orbit around the Earth, you are falling with everything else that surrounds you. Because the shuttle and everything in it is falling together, you float around in any direction. There is no up or down in space.

Soon it was time to get to work. Zac's job on the flight was to find out how animals are affected by being in orbit where gravity pulls them around Earth instead of against Earth.

He had rats and fish on board the shuttle and he needed to make sure they were all OK after the launch.

ARE YOU HUNGRY?

Hours later, Rory, the pilot, tapped Zac on the shoulder. Suddenly, he felt starving. He grinned at Rory and followed him to the galley.

Zac chose orange juice, fruit cocktail, beef with vegetbles, and chocolate pudding. He added water to each container and warmed up the beef in the oven.

MMMM . . . ALL MY FAVORITES!

To save storage space on the shuttle, most of the food and drink is dried and water is added before it is eaten. The water is squirted through a tube so none of it escapes and floats around the cabin.

When the food was ready, Zac put the containers on a tray along with his knife, fork, and spoon. Velcro strips held everything in place.

Zac strapped the tray to his knees. He had to make himself eat very slowly. If he grabbed at his food too fast it moved away from him!

It wasn't only the astronauts who were floating—everything else was, too. When Zac let go of his fork it stayed in midair until he got a hold of it again.

After a few days, Zac got used to life onboard the shuttle.

He learned how to sleep in a sleeping bag that was hung from a wall.

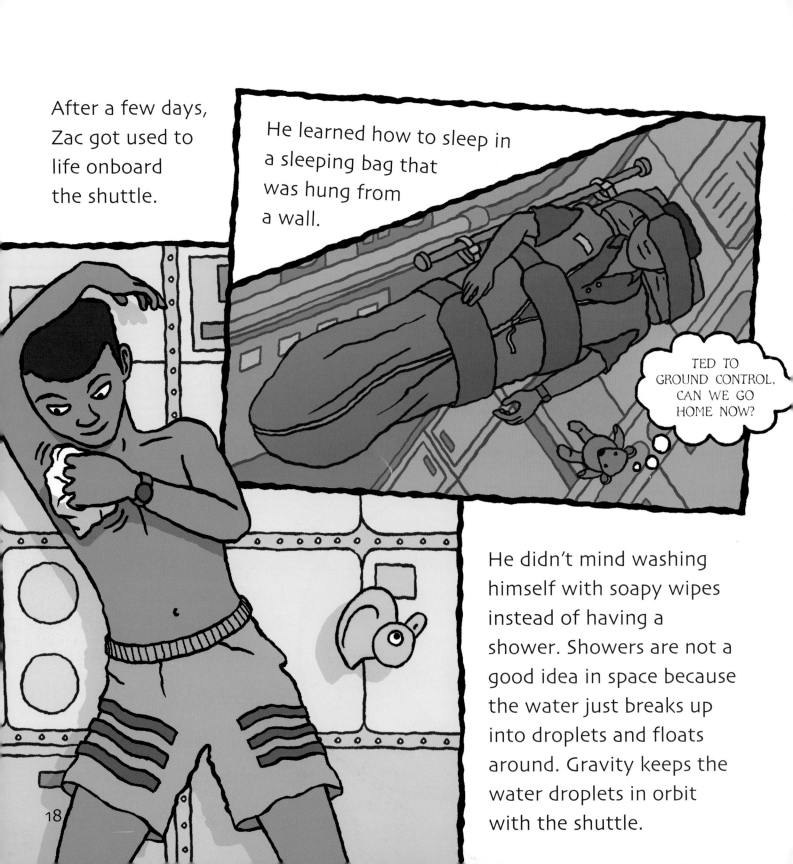

TED TO GROUND CONTROL, CAN WE GO HOME NOW?

He didn't mind washing himself with soapy wipes instead of having a shower. Showers are not a good idea in space because the water just breaks up into droplets and floats around. Gravity keeps the water droplets in orbit with the shuttle.

He got quite good at strapping himself onto the toilet with his feet on the footrests and two bars pulled across his legs.

EVEN USING THE BATHROOM IS CHALLENGING!

It is vital to stop waste or dirt floating about in a spacecraft. On the shuttle any solid or liquid waste goes straight into special containers and bags. It is stored and taken back to Earth.

WOW!

The one thing he never got used to was seeing Earth from space. He loved to watch the bright colors of his planet as it rolled beneath him.

Zac also liked looking at the moon. From the shuttle, he could clearly see the shadows and shapes on its shiny face.

The moon travels on an endless journey around and around the sun with its partner Earth. Earth's gravity keeps one side of the moon always facing us.

TIDE'S COMING IN!

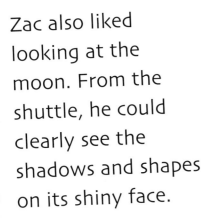

moon

Earth

The moon also pulls on Earth with the same strength that Earth pulls on the moon. It is the moon's gravity pulling on our oceans that makes the tides rise and fall.

Two weeks raced by, and Zac was amazed when it was time for the shuttle to return to Earth. Suddenly, everyone was busy cleaning up the crew areas and packing away their equipment.

WHERE DID ALL THIS STUFF COME FROM?

Zac strapped himself to his seat and took a last look at space. It sparkled with millions of stars like grains of sugar on a black tablecloth.

The shuttle dives back into the atmosphere. As the shuttle slows, gravity begins to pull the crew against their chairs.

WOW! THIS IS GETTING HOT!

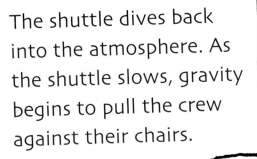

When something moves through air, it rubs against the stuff that air is made of. This rubbing action is called friction. The shuttle was falling so fast that friction made its surface glow red hot. It also slowed the shuttle down.

Rory guided the shuttle toward the landing site and everyone held their breath.

As the wheels touched the runway, a parachute billowed out behind it. Air filled the parachute and pushed it backward.

CAAAW!

The open parachute pulled against the shuttle, helping to slow it down before it reached the end of the runway.

Everyone cheered. They were glad to be safely home where they were familiar with the effects of gravity, but Zac knew that all of them would jump at the chance to go into space again.

# MORE GREAT STUFF TO KNOW

## RESISTING GRAVITY

Things fall because gravity pulls them downward, but not everything falls in the same way. A leaf floats gently to the ground, while an apple hits it with a thud. The pull of gravity alone would cause both of them to fall together, but the leaf falls more slowly because of its shape.

A leaf has a flat, thin shape. When it falls, it traps more air underneath it than the apple. The air pushes up against the leaf and slows it down. The air is resisting, or pushing against, the pull of gravity. If the apple was thin and flat like the leaf, it would fall slowly, too.

## STANDING UP

We use our bones and muscles to resist the pull of gravity. Without them we would not be able to lift ourselves off the ground. In space, an astronaut's body does not have to work against gravity. In fact, over time, astronauts can become as much as almost 2 inches (5 centimeters) taller in space because the bones in their spine spread out.

Astronauts exercise every day while they are in space. Otherwise their muscles would be too weak to hold them up when they got back to Earth.

24

## FLOATING ABOUT

Living in orbit takes some getting used to. Astronauts cannot eat bread or biscuits in space in case the crumbs float into a piece of machinery. Instead, they make their sandwiches from tortillas—a kind of chewy pancake.

Astronauts with long hair keep it tied firmly back. Otherwise it can float out around their head like seaweed in the ocean.

THIS IS MORE FUN THAN A TRAMPOLINE!

## MOONWALKING

All really massive objects have important pulls from gravity. The sun's gravity keeps Earth (and the moon) going around it once a year. On the moon, gravity pulled the astronauts down but, because the moon is smaller than Earth, they weigh six times less than they do on Earth—and they can jump six times higher.

# TRY IT AND SEE

## FLOATING ON AIR

How something falls on Earth depends on its shape. A crumpled ball of paper will fall faster than the same piece of paper when it's flat. This is because of the resistance of air. Parachutes use air resistance to slow an object's fall or to slow its speed along the ground.

**Try making your own toy parachutes to see how it works.**

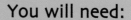
**You will need:**
- A plastic bag
- Cotton thread
- Some sticky tape
- A pair of scissors
- A ruler
- Some small plastic toys

**1** Cut two squares out of the plastic bag. Make one piece about 8 inches (20 cm) square and the other one about 12 inches (30 cm) square.

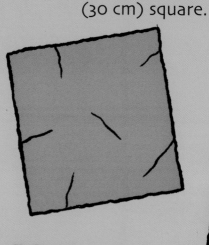

**2** Cut four lengths of thread for each square (that's eight lengths altogether). Make them all about 11 inches (28 cm) long.

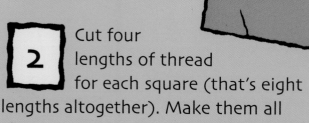

**3** Tape one thread to each corner of both squares. Make sure the tape is on the outside of the squares.

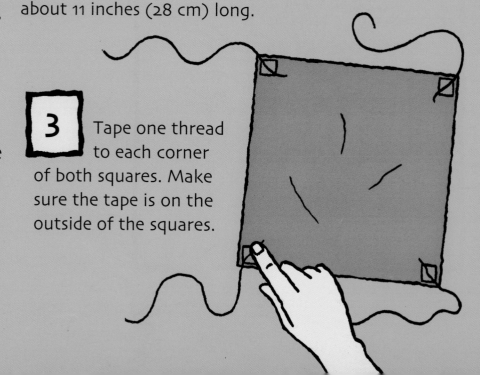

**4** Collect the ends of each set of four threads and loop them into a knot to keep them together.

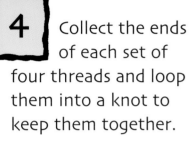

**5** Choose three plastic toys of roughly the same size and weight. Take two of the toys and tie or tape each one to the knotted end of a parachute.

**6** Take the two parachutes and the third toy to a safe high spot, such as the side of a staircase or stand on a sturdy chair. MAKE SURE AN ADULT IS WITH YOU. (If you are outside, it's best to do this when there is no wind, otherwise your parachutes could get blown away.)

First, drop the toy on its own. Count how long it takes to hit the ground. Now, drop each of the parchutes in turn. How long does each parachute take to land? Is there a difference between them?

The fastest to fall is the toy on its own. The slowest should be the largest parachute.

Try cutting a small hole in the top of one of the parachutes. Does this make a difference in how it falls?

WHO SAID PIGS CAN'T FLY!

27

# FORCEFUL FACTS

In space, any dust inside the shuttle just hangs in the air. It gets into the astronauts' eyes and makes them sneeze.

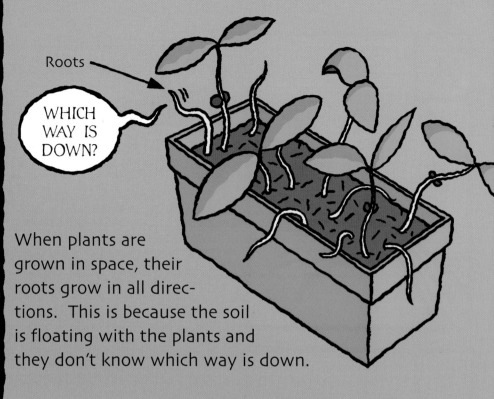

Roots

WHICH WAY IS DOWN?

When plants are grown in space, their roots grow in all directions. This is because the soil is floating with the plants and they don't know which way is down.

You are heavier at the North and South Poles than at the equator. This is because the Poles are slightly nearer to the center of the Earth. If you could stand at the center of Earth, you would be weightless.

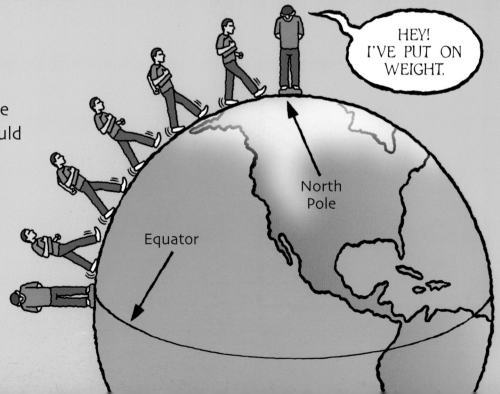

HEY! I'VE PUT ON WEIGHT.

North Pole

Equator

28

# GLOSSARY

**astronaut**—someone who travels in space

**atmosphere**—the gases that surround Earth

**boosters**—rockets that provide an extra thrust for the launching and initial part of the rocket's flight

**cope**—to deal with and attempt to overcome problems or difficulties

**friction**—the rubbing of one surface against another; friction stops or slows moving things and helps them start moving

**gravity**—the natural force that pulls things together and, also, toward Earth

## ON THE WEB

FactHound offers a safe, fun way to find Internet sites related to this book. All of the sites on FactHound have been researched by our staff.

1. Visit *www.facthound.com*

2. Type in this special code for age-appropriate sites: 140481597X

3. Click on the FETCH IT button.

   Your trusty FactHound will fetch the best sites for you!

# INDEX

## Read all of the books in the Science Works series:

A Drop in the Ocean:
The Story of Water
1-4048-0566-4

Charged Up:
The Story of Electricity
1-4048-0568-0

Cracking Up :
A Story About Erosion
1-4048-1594-5

Monster Bones:
The Story of a Dinosaur Fossil
1-4048-0565-6

The Rock Factory:
A Story of Rocks and Stones
1-4048-1596-1

Staying Alive:
The Story of a Food Chain
1-4048-1595-3

Sun Up, Sun Down:
The Story of Day and Night
1-4048-0567-2

Up, Down, All Around:
A Story of Gravity
1-4048-1597-X

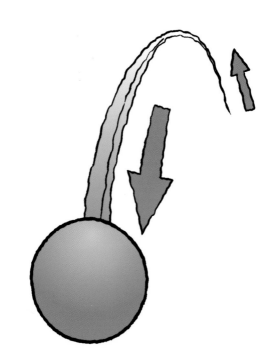